Teacher's Guide for

Kensie, Storyteller of Scotland

By Alice Lockmiller

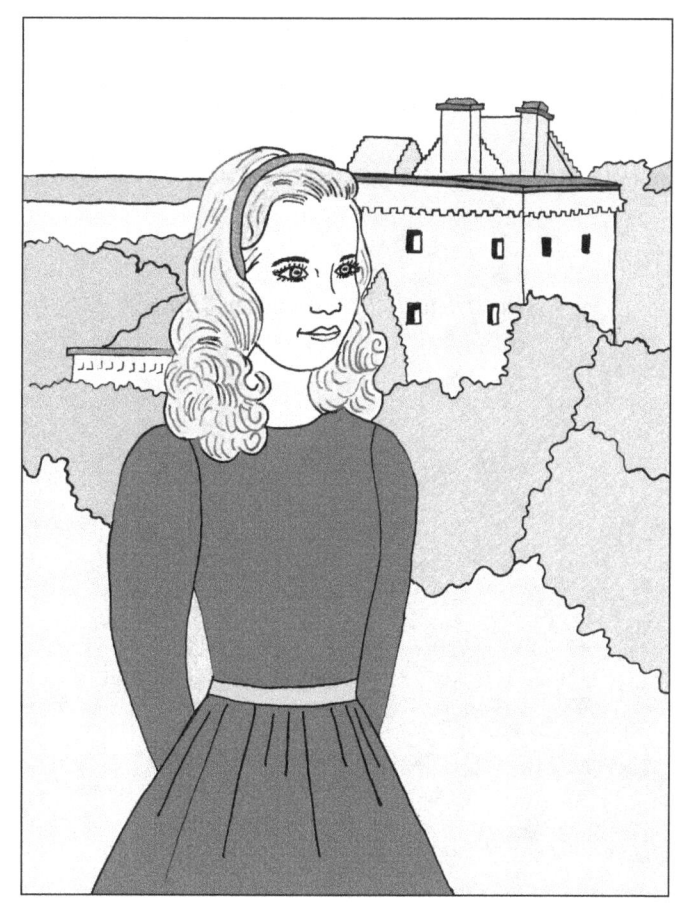

Printed in the United States of America

Layout and formatting by Charlotte Hamel

Illustrations by Alice Lockmiller

ISBN: 978-0-557-37386-4

Table of Contents

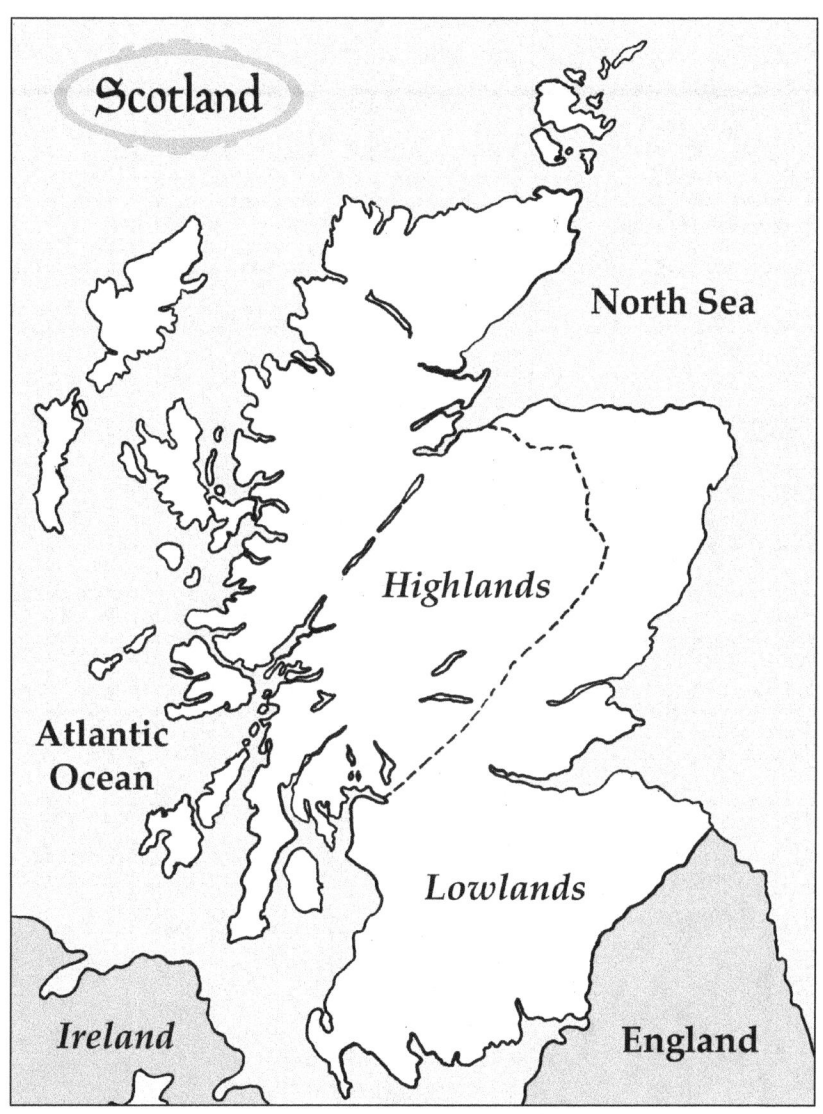

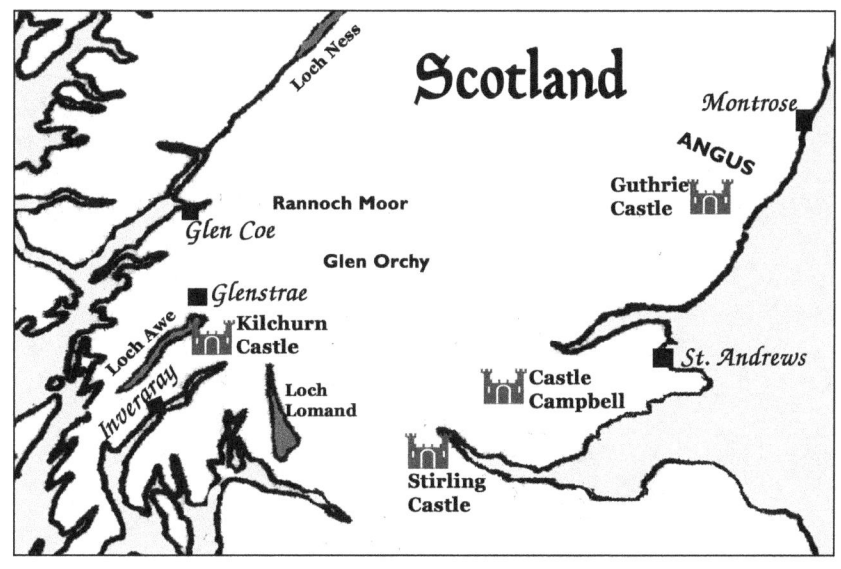

Scotland

Scotland is a country that occupies the northern third of the island of Great Britain. The North Sea is on the east and the Atlantic Ocean is on the north and west. In addition to the mainland, Scotland has over 790 islands.

Before the Dark Ages, the Kingdom of the Picts became the state called "Alba" or Scotland. These tattooed, tribal people joined together under common kings in response to Roman imperialism and were often considered pirates by Britannia (43-410 AD).

By the tenth century, the Pictish kingdom was occupied by the Gaelic people, from Ireland. (*Gaelic is a Celtic language.*) The name "Scotland" comes from the Latin "Scoti" (Gaels). In English, the Gaelic language was called "Scottis". "Scotia" (land of the Gaels) was the term used for the Galetic speaking Scotland north of the river Forth.

The people of the Lowlands, the southeastern part of Scotland, began speaking English (like their neighbors). In the north, the Highlands, the people retained the Gaelic language.

The Scottish Highlands include the rugged and mountainous regions of northwest Scotland, but exact boundaries are not clearly defined. The Highlands were different in land form, language and tradition. This was the home of many powerful clans and preserved Gaelic speech, customs and religion.

The United Kingdom

Scotland remained a separate independent state until 1707, but there was considerable conflict. England and Scotland fought many times for control of Scotland.

The former Prince of the Cumbrians (*the lowlands*), King David I (1085-1153), with his ties to England, began major changes in Scotland. The death of Alexander III in 1286 broke the succession line of Scotland's kings, opening the door to England's intervention.

Wars with England continued for several decades, bringing names like William Wallace and Robert the Bruce to notoriety. The Stewart Dynasty (*Jacobites*) followed, ruling Scotland for the rest of the Middle Ages.

In 1603, James VI, the King of Scots, inherited the throne of England. He became James I of England and left Edinburgh for London.

May 1, 1707, the Scots Parliament and the Parliament of England enacted the twin Acts of Union. This led to Scotland's formal incorporation into the Kingdom of Great Britain. Their laws, legislature, state church and education system have remained separate. But the Monarch of the UK (*e.g. the Queen*) is still the "head of state" in Scotland.

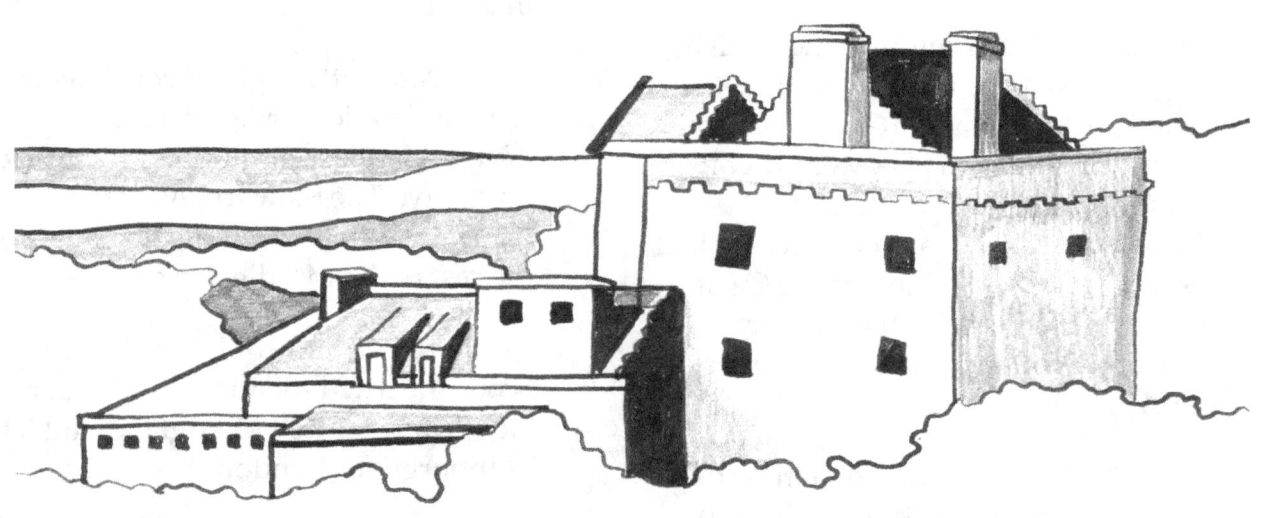

Castles of Scotland

Castles were first built in Scotland in the eleventh and twelfth centuries. The first stone castles appeared about 1200 and by 1400 the tower houses were popular. There have been over two thousand castles built in all parts of Scotland. Many are known only in historical records.

Castle Campbell

Castle Campbell sat in lofty isolation near the Ochil hills. These green woodland hills were at the head of Dollar Glen above the town of Dollar. The castle lifted out of a small forest of larch and beech trees and seemed to be inaccessible.

The approach to Castle Campbell was a rugged mountain path. A narrow road crossed a fearful chasm which partly surrounded the castle. It was crossed by a shaky wooden bridge. Two streams flowed in deep ravines around the castle.

Castle Campbell was once called *Castle of Gleume*. Tradition tells us the castle was given to Lady Mary Bruce Campbell on her marriage by her brother, King Robert the Bruce. The castle was isolated from the main body of Clan Campbell.

The buildings within Castle Campbell included a tower house, hall, chamber range, and east range. To the south were terraced gardens. The tower house had four main floors. An upper entrance was reached from the outside staircase and led into the hall.

The castle was attacked and burned in 1654. The castle was abandoned by the Campbell's, but they continued to own the lands.

Guthrie Castle

The Guthrie Castle is one of Scotland's most romantic castles. It is located near Forfar in Angus County between Edinburgh and Aberdeenshire. The original rectangular castle tower and entrance gate were built in 1468. It is a historic site and well known in Scotland.

The beautiful storybook castle has fifty-five rooms. It sits on the 156 acres of gorgeous lawns and has a two acre walled garden and a wildflower garden. It is known for the yew hedges shaped in the sign of the Celtic cross. Mysterious woods lead to the castle's own loch.

The castle was built by Sir David Guthrie (*treasurer to King James II*). It was only a square tower with walls fourteen feet thick. A house was built nearby around 1760. It also had its own separate chapel.

Like many Scottish castles, Guthrie is believed to be haunted. In 1620, the Bishop of St. Andrews said a ghost of the former Lady Guthrie came to make sure he was comfortable. Since then, she visits whoever is sleeping there.

Kensie Crossword

ACROSS

5 The songs Kensie sings are written as _____

7 Special animal Kensie saw in the forest

8 Kensie pretends her last name is _____

11 Kensie looks like a woman in a _____

14 The town near Castle Campbell

16 Two famous Guthrie ministers were William and _____

17 Kensie played a Gaelic harp called a _____

18 King of England and Scotland at the time of the story

19 Kensie has a recurring _____ that scares her.

20 Famous hero of Scotland and portrait in Guthrie Castle

DOWN

1 Castle where Angus lives

2 Erica gave Kensie a beautiful blue _____

3 Kensie helped cook the _____ for Hogmanay.

4 The Covenanters were led by _____ _____

6 Famous king of Scotland who saw a spider

9 The mountainous part of Scotland is called the _____

10 A dark-haired stranger who arrives just after midnight is a _____ _____

12 The Campbell colors are blue and _____.

13 A misty place where the MacGregor's lived

15 Erica comes to Kensie's room through a secret _____

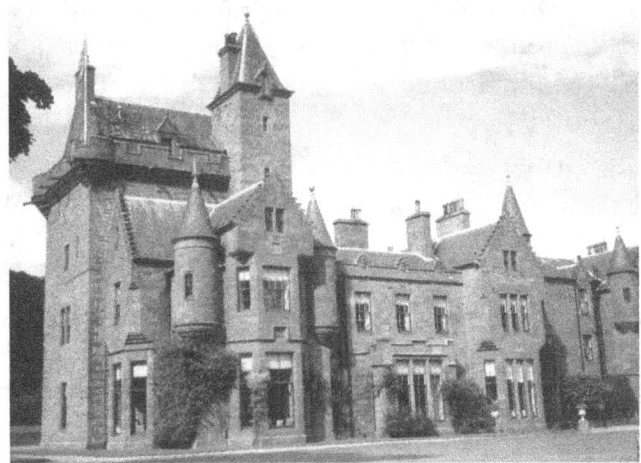

Guthrie Castle today

Kensie Crossword

NAME: _____ DATE: _____

Highland Clans

Clan in Gaelic means "children" or "family". The clan system was a tribal civilization and claimed descent from noble, royal or even mythological ancestors. When the Romans left Britain, the tribes divided themselves into four kingdoms. Dalriada was the kingdom of Celtic Scots; Strathclyde was the Britons; the Lowlands was the Angles or Saxons; and the north was the Picts. The Scots and Picts later united to form the kingdom of Alba (Scotia).

Under the Celtic system, land belonged to the tribe. Under feudalism, all land belonged to the king, who could distribute it at will. The Scottish king was somewhere between a monarch and a chief. The chief was an equal in the clan but also an unchallenged leader.

The Highlanders were divided into tribes or clans under chiefs or chieftains. Each clan was divided into branches (septs) who had chieftains over them. These were subdivided into smaller branches of fifty or sixty men. They relied on the original chief for protection and defense. The clansmen loved their chief and give him blind obedience. Next to the love of the chief was love of their branch and then to the whole clan or name.

They also supported other friendly clans. Finally, they supported other highlanders in opposition to the Lowlanders. Tradition told them the Lowlands were their possession in old times.

The power of the chief came from his line of ancestors – the old patriarchs or fathers of families. He was bound to protect his followers even against laws. There were hereditary feuds between clans which had been handed down from one generation to another for several ages.

The Highland clans developed into independent units that would identify and distinguish their society. The Highlands also developed as a region of scattered communities with a separate language and culture. When Robert the Bruce established himself as king of a united Scotland (1306), he gave land and power to those who supported him. Many of these became strong and developed their own ideas.

England always believed it had superiority over Scotland. In the north, clan disputes and squabbles also continued. In 1603, the crowns of England and Scotland were united under James, but the Highland clans had become very remote from government. Some leaders and rulers understood the fighting abilities of the Highland clans and were able to rally and employ them successfully.

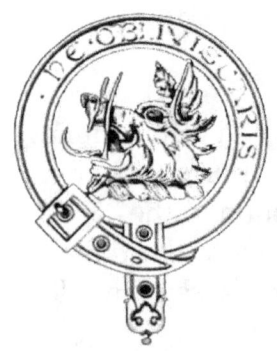

Campbell

The name Campbell seems to come from the Gaelic "cam-beul" which means "crooked mouth". The Campbells are a large, wealthy and powerful Scottish clan and one of the oldest in the highlands. The original documented Campbell chief was Sir Colin (Cailein) of Loch Awe who died in 1294, but tradition follows the clan back many generations earlier.

The Campbells were described by many as devious and cunning and others as clever and polite. The success of Clan Campbell was based on support of the winning side, usually the government. They supported Robert the Bruce and later the Stewart dynasty. The clan expanded steadily and took advantage of feuds and failure in other clans. They always secured legal title to lands or charters from the Crown and used force if necessary.

The Campbells of the story are the Campbells of Argyll, the Chiefly House and the Campbells of Glenarchy (Breadalbane). These are two of the four branches of the clan. The motto of the Campbells of Argyll is "ne obliviscaris" which means "lest you forget". The motto of the Campbells of Breadalbane is "follow me." The symbol on the crests is a boar which represents power and strength.

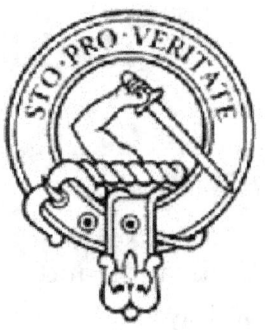

Guthrie

The Guthrie name is said to come from Guthrum, a Scandinavian prince who settled in Scotland in the dawn of Scottish history. Early Guthries were royal falconers. In 1299, Squire Guthrie was sent to France to bring William Wallace back to continue fighting the English.

The Guthries of Guthrie received their estates by a charter from King David II of Scotland between the years 1329 and 1371. They were a Lowland clan, with holdings in the south eastern part of Scotland.

They supported young King James VI against his mother, Mary Queen of Scots. But during the time of Martin Luther, the Guthries also supported the reformed religion in Scotland (*Presbyterianism*).

James Guthrie (from the story) was a minister and supported the Convenanters. When he moved to Stirling in 1649, he preached openly against the king's religious views. He was arrested and executed in 1661.

The Guthrie clan tartan is blue-gray and dark blue check with an orange over-check. The Guthrie Motto is "Sto pro-veritate" which means "I stand for truth."

MacGregors

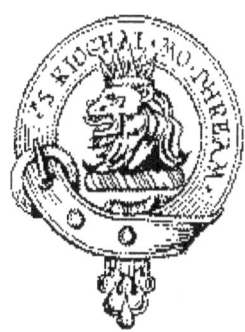

"Royal is my Race" (*'S rioghal mo dhream*) is the motto of this ancient Scottish clan (ca 800 AD). The clan claimed descent from Griogar, the third son of King Alpin of Dalriada (*whose father married a Pict Princess*). He ascended the Celtic Scottish throne about 787. Their crest is a lion's head with a crown.

Glenurchy was the original seat of the Clan Gregor, but they later possessed many other territories. These lands were held by right of first occupation or the "right of the sword." But they did have the title deeds.

The Campbells became a powerful clan and managed to get Crown charters for many of these MacGregor lands. Robert the Bruce even granted the barony of Loch Awe to the Campbells, confining the MacGregor clan to Glenstrae.

In 1440 bands of MacGregors took refuge in Rannoch because they had been driven out of their ancestral lands. These lands of Glen Orchy were the ancient home of the MacGregors

The MacGregors tried to hold these lands by the sword, since their ancestors had won them that way. The clan acquired a reputation for turbulence and robbery throughout Scotland.

(The Proscription) Acts were passed by the Scottish Parliament against the unfortunate clan. In 1603, they were commanded to change their name under pain of death. They could not carry weapons and no more than four members of the clan could meet together.

The change of name was also for future generations. Many MacGregors adopted other names such as Campbell, Grant, Murray and Stewart. In 1633 an act declared it unlawful for any man to bear the name of MacGregor.

There could be no signature bearing that name and no agreement with a MacGregor was legal. A MacGregor could be killed without punishment and no minister could baptize a male child of a MacGregor. The Proscription was finally lifted in 1774.

Rob Roy MacGregor (using the name Campbell) was a younger son of MacGregor of Glengyle. He took part in the first Jacobite uprising in 1715 and was made famous by Sir Walter Scott.

Stories of mountains, lochs, and rivers are interwoven in Scottish legends of the clans. Many legends tell of the MacGregors of Rannoch Moor. It is a wild stretch of country when shrouded in mist. It is on the north side of Loch Rannoch. From this land, the MacGregors were named the "Children of the Mist."

People Have Feelings

NAME: _____ DATE: _____

Kensie had many different feelings about the situations in her life.

Put an X in the box or boxes that best describe the feelings you might have for each situation below.

How would you feel if you:	Important	Happy	Sad	Afraid	Excited	Good	Nervous	Proud	Worried
were left in a strange castle									
watched your parents leave you									
were told to use another last name									
knew your parents were probably dead									
wrote your first verse to sing									
met a new friend									
lied to people about who you really were									
sang your verses in front of a crowd									
made your first haggis									
saw a beautiful white stag									
saw a portrait that looked like you									
walked outside in a beautiful place									

Tartans

Tartan means "checked or with stripes crossing each other at right angles". The tartan plaids evolved by tradition to become the universally accepted national dress of Scotland. The tartans are a recognized symbol of pride and were very important in Scotland's cultural identity. Striped cloth was worn at an early stage, but the first to reference the tartan was in 1538.

The wool for tartan cloth was from the long, fine fleece of the Highland sheep. It was ideal for spinning into fine hard thread using a spindle by the women of the glen. Colors came from the various plants in the area. These women worked hard to create an exact pattern of plaid in the wool. The pattern became associated with a clan because it was made in their territory.

The favorite colors were purple and blue, though dark brown was good when hiding in heather on the moors. The raw wool was soaked in human urine to remove grease and it acted as a fixing agent for the colors. Then it was washed and dried. After spinning the wool, the skeins were simmered in a pot with dye plants until it achieved the desired color. It was virtually impossible to exactly match colors.

There was a close relation between heraldry and clanship and the tartans gained clan significance. Use of the same colors showed clans had a similar origin. Making of tartans was a simple craft industry and the skill was passed from mother to daughter

The Scottish Kilt

The Scottish kilt is the belted plaid worn by Scottish men. The plaid is a huge blanket of tartan cloth, about five feet wide and twelve to eighteen feet long. It was made of two strips 30 inches wide and sewn down the length.

The cloth is laid out on the ground and pleated to a length of four or five feet. A couple of feet are left un-pleated at either end. The wearer lies down on the plaid and the un-pleated ends are wrapped across the front of his body. It is belted at the waist.

The plaid is pleated over the belt. After the wearer stands, he drapes the top half around his body. The plaid is draped over one shoulder or both. It can also be pulled over his head in bad weather.

The close weave of the plaid made it moderately waterproof. The plaid served as a sleeping bag when out in the open at night as well as a convenient daytime garment.

In addition to belted plaids, tartan wool was used to make tight-fitting pants and stockings in one piece. These were tartan trews. They were tied with an elaborate garter which was wound around the leg and secured with a garter knot.

The men of Scotland also wore saffron shirts, short woolen jackets and leather shoes.

Design a Plaid

<u>MATERIALS</u>

Colored pencils or watercolor paint   paintbrush

Copy of plaid sheet (copy on cardstock for paint)

<u>STEPS:</u>

To make the plaid for the Campbells of Breadalbane, follow the following color codes on the diagram in this sequence:

- Color all yellow lines (Y) vertically and horizontally

- Color vertical lines: (L) = light blue, (D) = Dark blue, (G) = green

- Color the horizontal lines as coded.

To design your own plaid, choose three or four colors and follow the order above to color the lines.

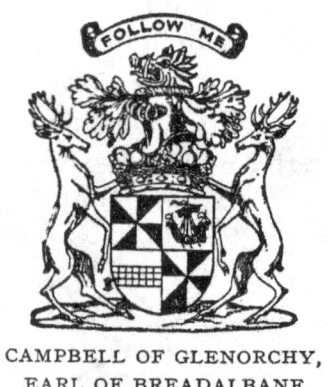

CAMPBELL OF GLENORCHY,
EARL OF BREADALBANE

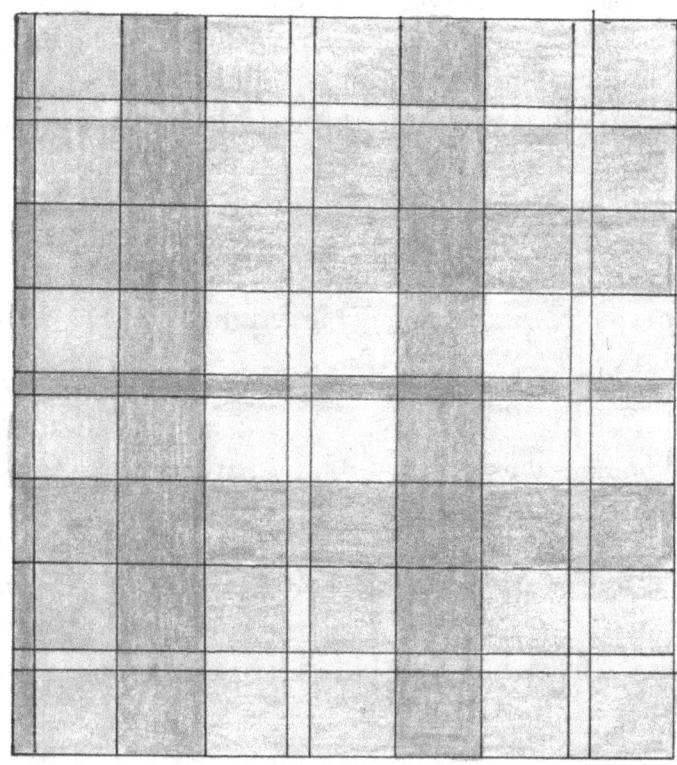

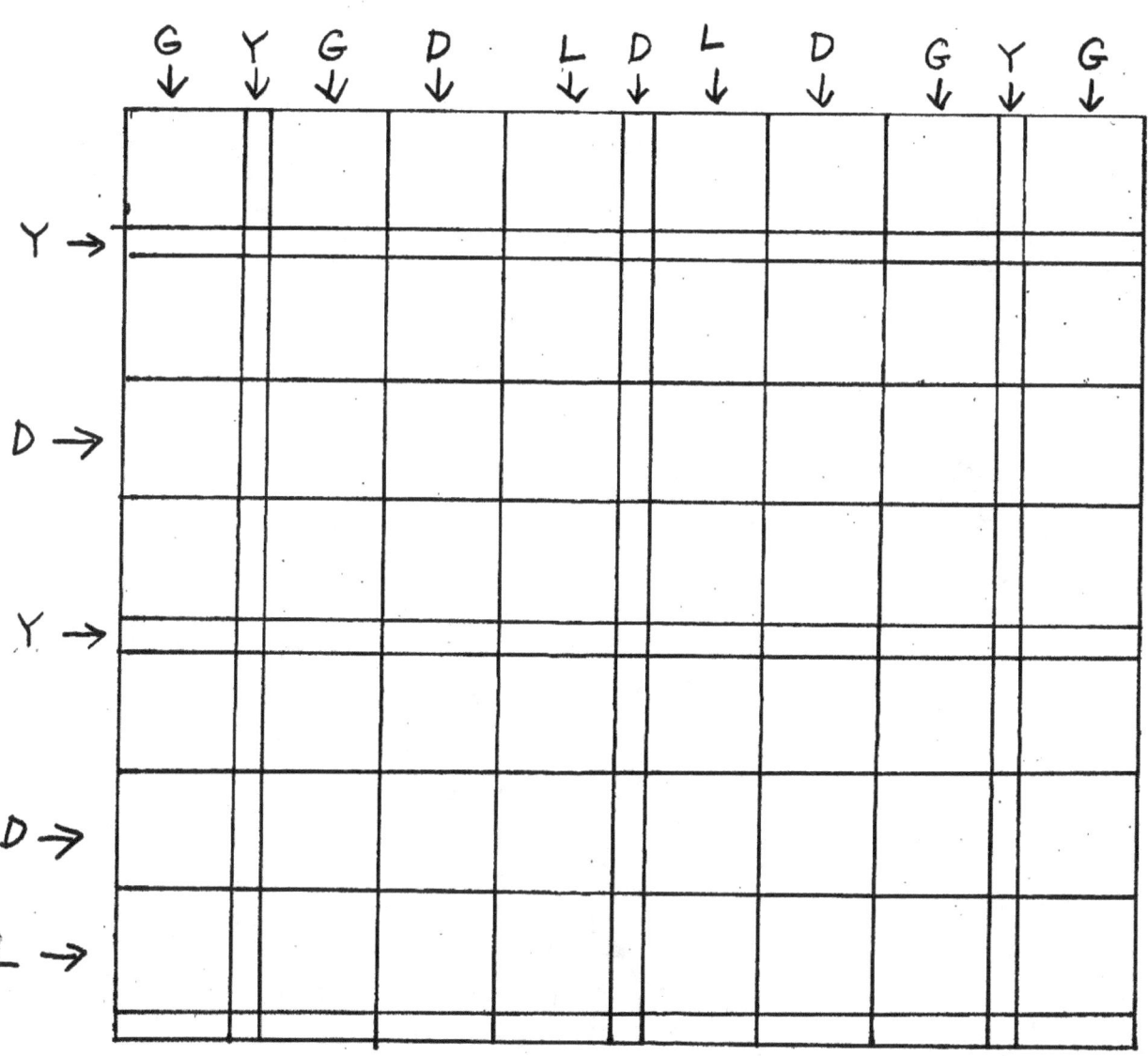

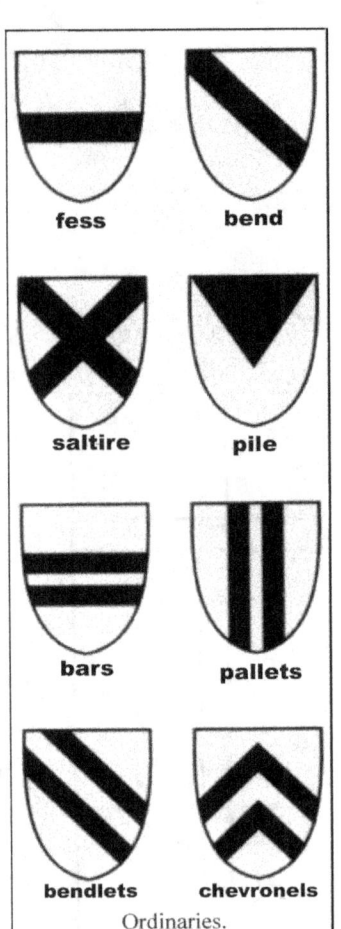

fess   bend

saltire   pile

bars   pallets

bendlets   chevronels

Ordinaries.

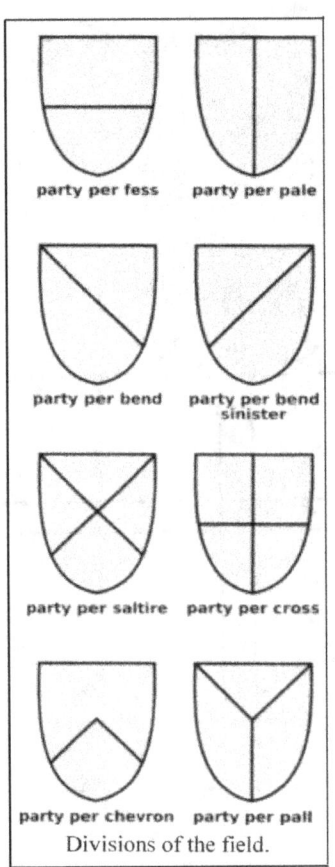

party per fess   party per pale

party per bend   party per bend sinister

party per saltire   party per cross

party per chevron   party per pall

Divisions of the field.

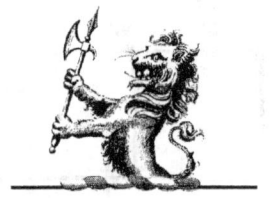

FURS

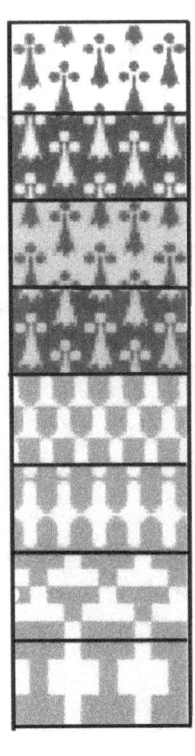

Ermine
(black on white)

Ermines
(white on black)

Erminois
(black on gold)

Pean
(gold on black)

ermine

Vair
(white on color)

Counter-vair
(white on color, joined two together at bottoms)

vair

Potent
(white on color)

potent

Counter-potent
(color on white, joined two together at bottoms)

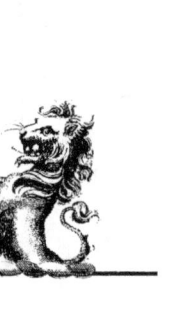

Heraldry

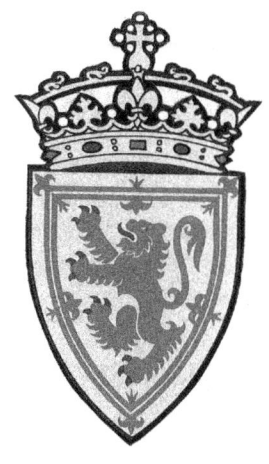

heraldry is the practice of designing, displaying, describing and recording coats of arms and badges. The origins of its history lie in the need to distinguish men in combat when helmets hid their faces. A standard system of rules developed into the modern form of heraldry in the middle twelfth century, but some rules differed from country to country.

Coats of arms were inherited by the children in many families across Europe. In Britain, the practice of using "marks of cadency" distinguished one son from another. Coats of arms were displayed in castles, carved on family tombs and flown as a banner in country homes.

A variety of media have been used to produce coats of arms. These include paper, wood, embroidery, enamel, stonework and stained glass. Each element of the coat of arms could have originally had specific meaning, but the meaning was not often retained from generation to generation.

Description of the elements of a coat of arms used a language called blazon. "Tinctures" were the colors used in heraldry.

Many charges (*objects*) in their natural colors, or "proper", were also called tinctures. Colors were azure (blue), gules (red), sable (black) vert (green) and purpure (purple).

Metals (lighter tinctures) could never be placed on metals or colors placed on colors. Metals were gold and argent (white). A number of patterns called furs were used. Two common furs were ermine and vair (two colored).

The field of a shield in heraldry could be divided into more than one tincture. In the early days of heraldry, very simple bold shapes, called ordinaries, were used. These included the cross, fess (*broad horizontal band*), pale (*vertical stripe*), bend, chevron, saltire (*diagonal cross*), and pall (*Y shape*).

A charge is any object or figure placed on a heraldic shield. Charges could be animals, objects or geometric shapes. The most frequent charges were crosses, eagles and lions. Other common charges were stags, boars, fish, dragons, unicorns and griffins.

On a Scottish coat of arms, the shield is tilted to the left and a helmet with a mantle sits on top. (*The mantle was originally a cloth worn over the back of a helmet to protect from heat and sunlight.*) An animal or object is on top of the helmet. The motto is written on a ribbon at the top of the crest.

Make a Coat of Arms

MATERIALS

White cardstock   pencil

Acrylic paint   brush

STEPS:

1. Copy the Campbell coat of arms on cardstock OR draw your own.

2. Paint the coat of arms using correct colors

3. If you are Scottish, find your own coat of arms online or in a book at the library.

4. If you design your own, use the information from Heraldry to help you with the design.

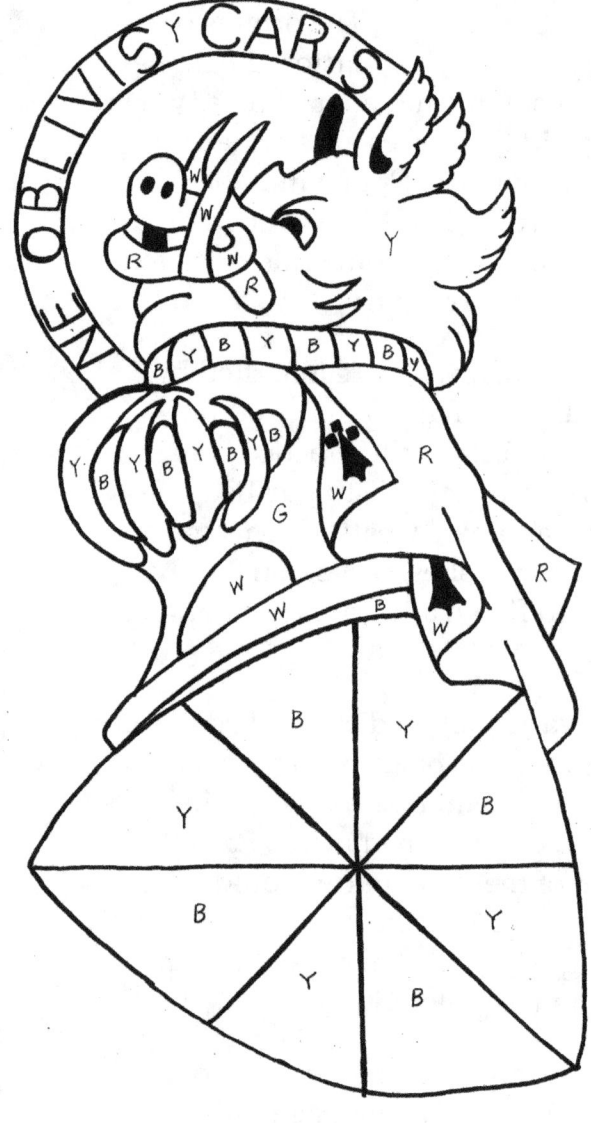

Color code for
Campbell coat of
arms

    Y = yellow
    R = red
    B = black
    W = white

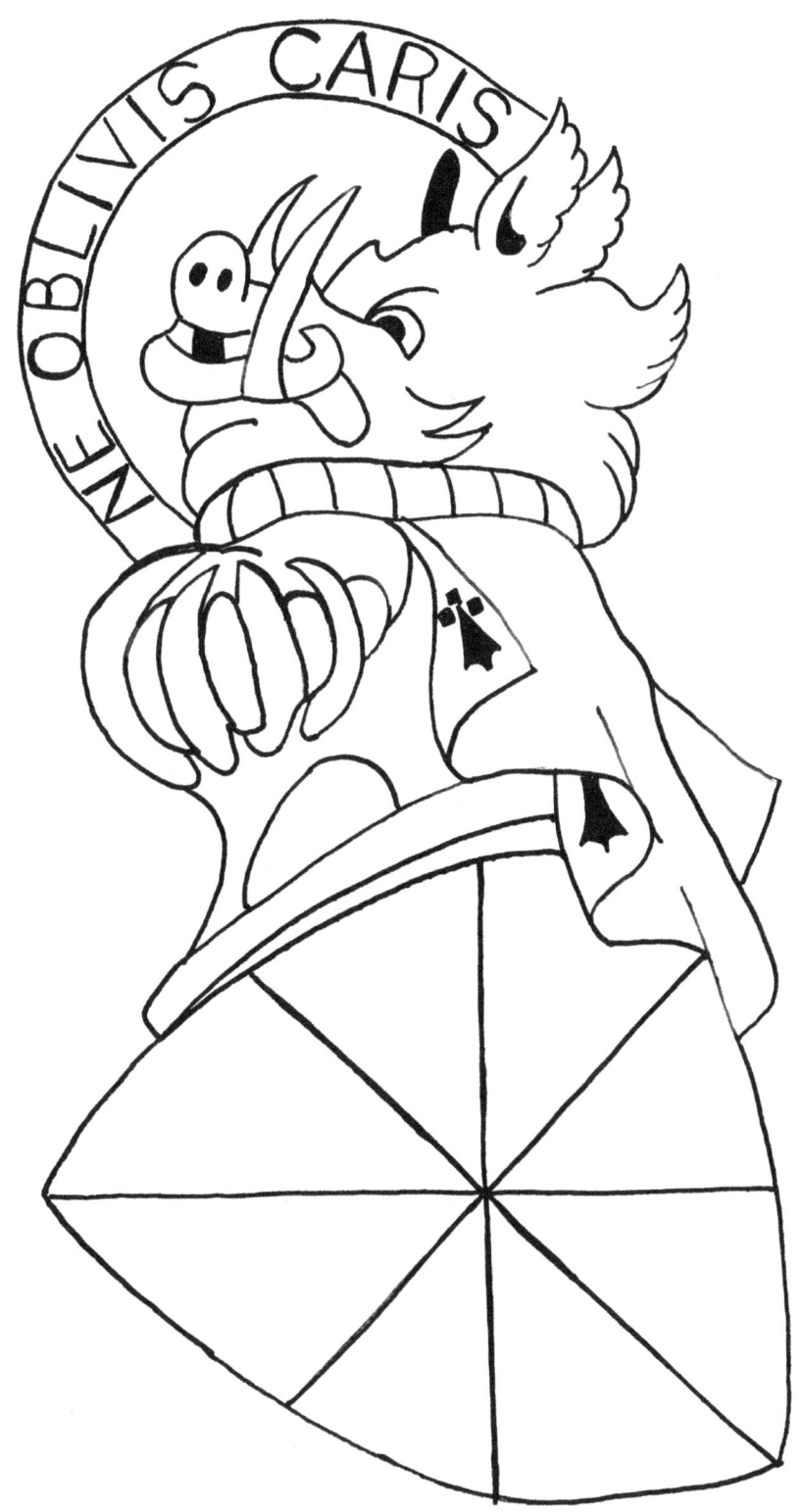

The Covenanters

Covenanters took their name from the Biblical bonds called covenants. The group opposed the Episcopal Church favored by the King of England and promoted the development of Presbyterianism as a form of church government which had more democratic elements and was favored by the people. Documents were proposed and signed between the Covenanters of Scotland and the King and Parliament of England.

In a series of bonds or covenants, the Covenanters bound themselves to maintain the Protestant Reformation in Scotland (*the Scottish break with the Papacy in 1560*). The ideas of the Reformation in Scotland were based on Calvinism. It is a theological system and approach to Christian life that emphasizes the rule of God over all things.

King James (early 17th century) attempted, but did not succeed in creating a unified state or a unified church. Then came Charles I and his Act of Revocation, which threatened to rob the Scottish nobles of the church land they had previously gained. Charles questioned the teachings of the Scottish church, undermined the political power of the aristocracy, and gave power to the bishops of his church (Church of England).

Charles turned a protest into a rebellion. Protestors answered the King with a National Covenant and his enemies became the Covenanters. Their leader was Archibald Campbell, acting head of the powerful Clan Campbell. Wars were fought for religion in England, Ireland and Scotland for 12 years.

The Covenanters supported the Church of Scotland, called the Kirk. It broke with Rome and reformed its doctrine and government. This church had no prayer book, as the Catholics and Episcopalians did. Hymns, prayers and preaching were the central focus of most services. The church traces its roots to these early Christians in Scotland and became a national church (*the Church of Scotland*).

The Kirk maintains a presence in every community in Scotland today. It exists to serve its members and all Scots. The church played a leading role in providing universal education in Scotland, so all people could read the Bible.

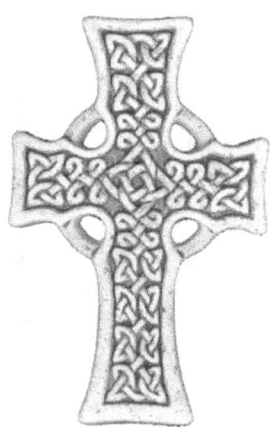

Early form of Ionic (Celtic) cross adopted by the Presbyterians

Flag of the Church of Scotland

MATERIALS
Colored pencils or crayons
Copy of the flag

Colors of the flag
Shaded areas – orange
Flames on tree – yellow
Tree leaves – green
Tree trunk – brown
Inside with points behind
tree – white
Outside points – yellow

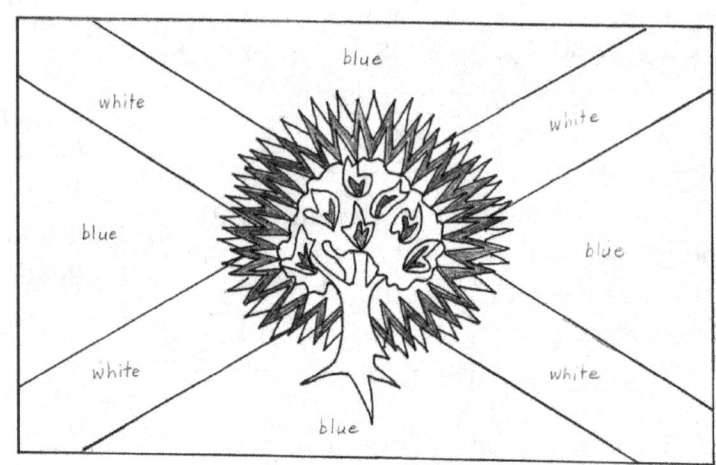

**What do you think is the meaning
of the picture on the flag?**

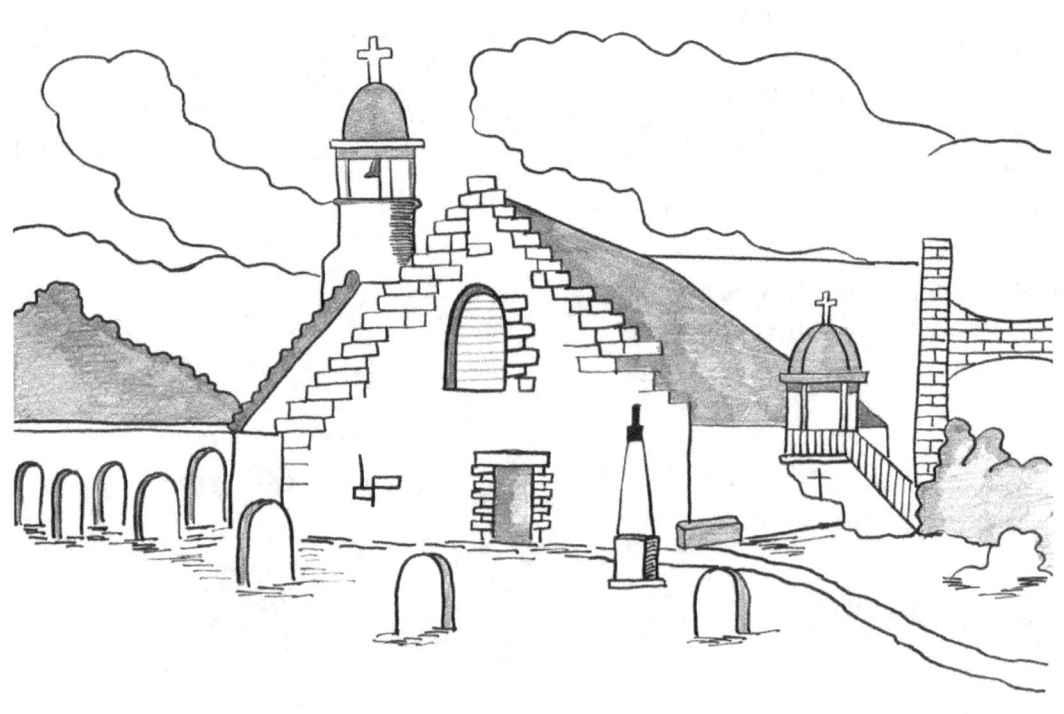

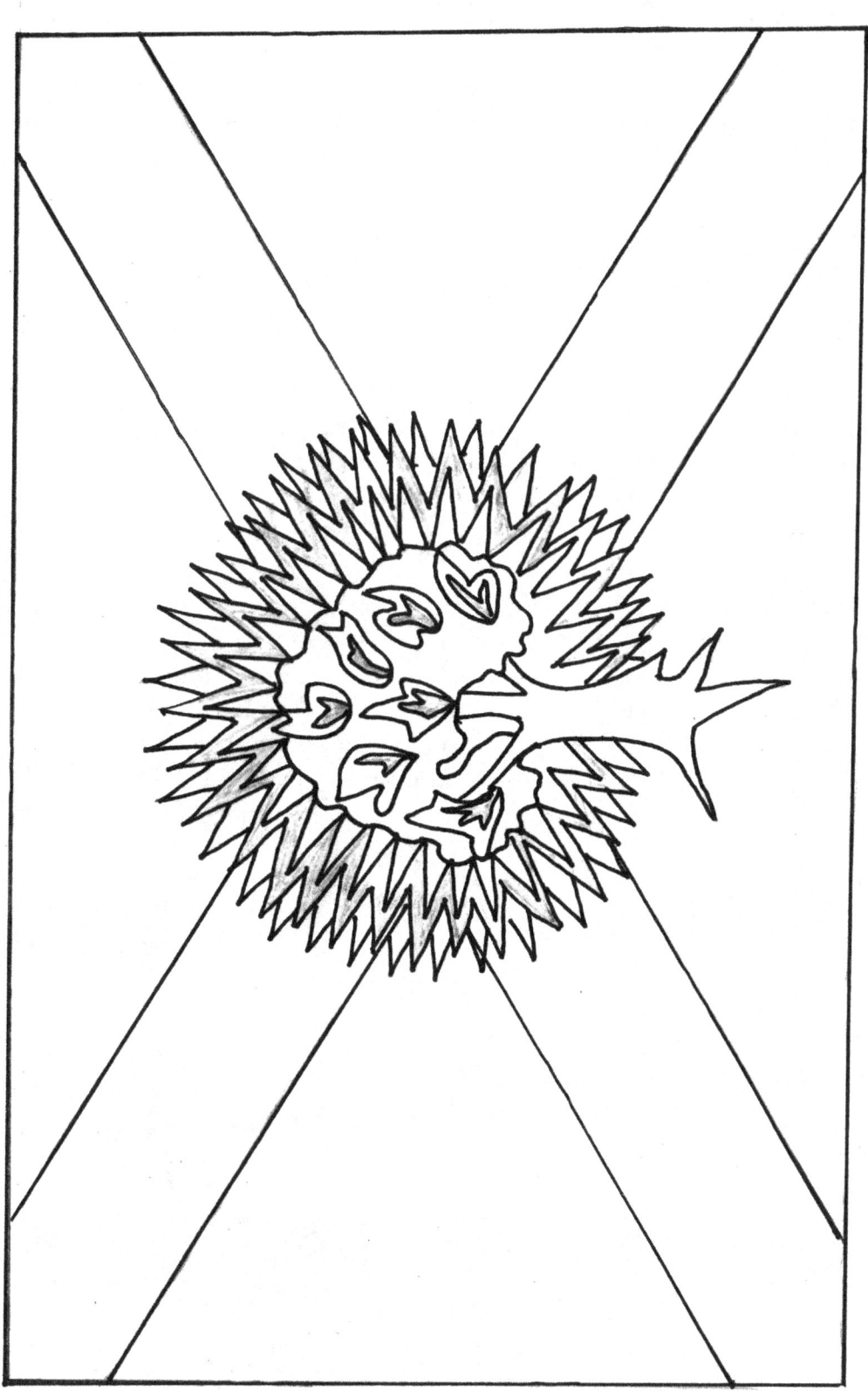

Hogmanay

hogmanay (*hógmə náy* or *hug-m'NAY*) is one of the most celebrated events in Scottish history. It is believed the name came from the Gaelic "oge maidne" meaning "new morning". It is the celebration of New Years Eve and the midwinter festival. It also comes from ancient Scandinavian/ Norse roots in the Yule festival.

Hogmanay is the festival at the end of winter and a celebration of survival of the dark misery of this cold season. Presbyterians in Scotland scarcely celebrated Christmas, but they did celebrate Hogmanay. The custom of singing *Auld Lang Syne (Robert Burns Poem, 1788)* came from Hogmanay festivals.

The day before the New Year dawns is a time of reckoning, atonement and balancing the books of life. Debts and dirt belong to the old times and should not be carried into the New Year. Debts are settled and houses are thoroughly cleaned. New Years resolutions are made.

A few minutes before midnight the ashes are raked from under the fire and removed from the house. Finally, the bells strike signifying Balder has risen from the dead.

The First Foot

Soon after midnight, other Scotsmen venture into the black night. They are called the First Foot. These men are emissaries of the ancient gods to bring the blessing of prosperity to neighbors.

The First Foot must be male and should be dark haired and bearing proper gifts. He must carry a small drink (dram) of spirits, to give to the family and receive one in return. He should carry Black Bun (*rich, moist fruitcake in pastry*).

Legend of Balder

Balder is the Norse god of light. He was killed by an arrow of mistletoe. His mother, Frigg, had sworn all things on Earth not to harm him, but overlooked the mistletoe as unimportant. Balder didn't die permanently, but rose again in the spring.

**Mistletoe was thought to once be a tree, from which the wood of Christ's cross was formed.

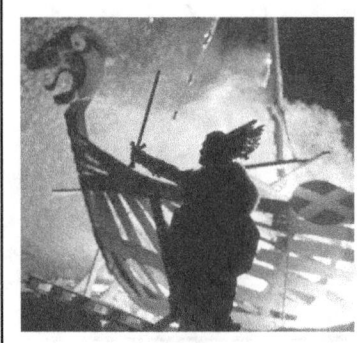

Viking fires became Scottish torches and later fireworks.

Compare and Contrast

MATERIALS

Notebook paper and pencil

STEPS:

1. Hogmanay is the Scottish New Years Eve. Read the information in the guide and the book about the festival. You may also want to go online.

2. Make a list of everything you learned about Hogmanay.

3. Ask your parents and other people how they celebrate New Years Eve.

4. Make another list including the following:

   - special foods
   - special songs
   - kinds of dancing
   - instruments played
   - what is done just before and/or just after midnight
   - people you celebrate with
   - decorations
   - special words/ greetings

5. Use the information from both lists to compare and contrast Hogmanay and New Years Eve.

   * **Compare** is how two things are alike/ similar.

   * **Contrast** is how two things are different.

6. Determine which one you like best and why.

7. Write at least three paragraphs using your information.

Bards

Bards of Scotland were professional poets attached to the courts of chiefs. A bard sang the praises of the chief. They also inspired clansmen on the eve of battle or to celebrate victories.

The bard used a classical language that was not used by common people. Bardic poems were intricate, ornate compositions and often repeated in the same words from one generation to another. The poems chronicled the chief's heroic deeds and those of his clansmen or the history of Scotland.

Ceilidhs

Ceilidh was a special celebration held by the light of the peat-fire flame on winter evenings. Songs, poetry and legendary epics were performed by bards and storytellers. They used a particular kind of harp called a clarsach. The songs and verses were sung as the storyteller played the clarsach. There was good food, singing and dancing.

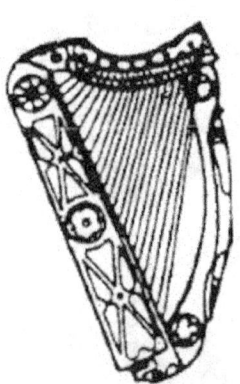

Clarsach. Source www.harpsglasgow.com

Write a Verse

Kensie wrote verses to perform at Ceilidhs and other events. Read some of the verses in the book again and try writing verses of your own.

MATERIALS

Notebook paper and pencil

STEPS:

Think of something you learned about Kensie (or another character) or about Scotland.

Follow this basic form to write your verse:

       Line 1 seven syllables

       Line 2 six syllables

       Line 3 seven syllables

       Line 4 six syllables

The last word in Line 2 rhymes with the last word in Line 4.

*You may want to make a list of rhyming words first – maybe 4 or 5 sets.

One of the words could be something about Scotland. Remember some words are very hard to rhyme.

Talk About the Story

1. How did Blaire know Kensie was not a Guthrie?

2. What was the lump of coal supposed to do? Did it work?

3. Why do you think Kensie likes to be outside?

4. What is a feud? Why do groups of people have feuds?

5. What is a clarsach? What was different about the one at Kilchurn Castle?

6. Why did Kensie know so much about haunted castles? Did she believe in ghosts?

7. What two things does Lady Davina say Kensie must be? Which was more important? Why?

8. Why were Kensie's parents being hunted? Will they come back? If so, where have they been?

9. Can anyone be a poet and a storyteller? What special skills do you think it takes?

10. If Kensie were not a storyteller, what do you think she would be? Why did you make that choice?

11. Why was Castle Campbell attacked? Why did they kill only the boys?

12. There are three castles in the story. Which one do you like best? Give three reasons.

13. Why couldn't Angus be a First Foot?

14. What is special about a white stag? Why do you think Kensie saw one?

15. Kensie kept having the same dream. What was it? Did it really happen?

16. What is Hogmanay? How was it celebrated?

17. Will Kensie marry Angus? What will she be doing in five years? In ten years?

18. Why do you think Lady Davina accepted Kensie even though she knew she was a MacGregor? Did John accept her? How do you know?

Write and Draw About the Story

1. A man named <u>Montrose</u> was mentioned several times in the story. Research the name. Who was he? What did he do?

2. The Covenanters were Presbyterian. Research <u>Presbyterianism</u>. What special beliefs do they have?

3. Using the information in the story, write a recipe for seaweed soup or haggis.

4. Use the descriptions in the story to draw Castle Campbell, Guthrie Castle, Kilchurn Castle or Blaire's house.

5. Use **Two Friends – Alike or Different?** worksheet to write about Erica and Blaire.

6. Complete the sheet **What Did They Do?** to determine character reactions to Kensie's secret.

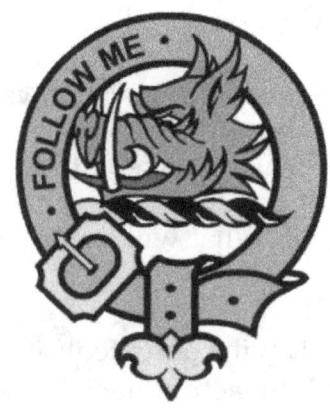

Two Friends – Alike or Different?

NAME: _____ DATE _____

Kensie had two friends in the story. Were they alike or different? Use the Venn Diagram to show how they were alike and how they were different.

Words about Erica

Words about Erica and Blaire

Words about Blaire

Which part has the most words? _____

Were they alike or different? _____

In five years, will Kensie still be friends with Erica, Blaire or both?

_____

Why? _____

_____

What Did They Do?

NAME: _____ **DATE** _____

Explore the way several characters in <u>Kensie, Storyteller of Scotland</u> reacted when they learned Kensie's secret. In each box list a character, the way in which he or she reacted to the information, and why.

Character 1 _____	Character 2 _____
Character 3 _____	Character 4 _____

What Did They Do? Continued.

Which character reacted most appropriately considering the circumstances?

_____ because _____

_____

_____

_____

_____

Which character's reaction was most like YOU probably would have reacted to

the secret? _____ because _____

_____

_____

_____

_____

Review: Do You Know?

NAME: _____ DATE _____

1. The only thing Kensie had from her parents was her _____.

2. Color of Kensie' hair _____

3. Former name of Castle Campbell was Castle _____.

4. Many castles in Scotland are _____.

5. The main room of a castle is the _____ _____.

6. James Guthrie is a minister for the religious group called the
   _____.

7. Kensie's real last name is _____.

8. Kensie's friend at Castle Campbell was _____.

9. Festival with singing and dancing is a _____.

10. New Year's Eve celebration is called _____.

11. Angus played the _____

12. Kensie wants to be a _____.

13. The first thing Kensie cooks at Castle Campbell is _____ soup.

14. Scottish plaid is called _____.

15. A special food served at the New Year feast was _____.

16. The First Foot gave Kensie a piece of _____.

17. A Scottish lake is called a _____.

18. A person who sees the future was called _____.

19. Kensie writes poems called _____.

20. James brought Kensie a _____ that belonged to her mother.

It Happened in Time

Each Teacher's Guide for this series of Historical Fiction has information to add to a timeline. If you made a timeline, add these events to the timeline:

<u>Timeline List</u>

379 AD	First Christian Church in Scotland
1270-1305 AD	William Wallace, Scottish patriot
1274-1329 AD	Robert the Bruce (*he became king of Scotland*)
1314 AD	Bannockburn, Scots victory over English
1560 AD	John Knox's Reformed Church begins in Scotland
1560 AD	The Geneva Bible; first Bible printed with verse divisions
1603 AD	James became James I of England and James VI of Scotland
1607 AD	Proclamation made it illegal to bear the name MacGregor
1611 AD	King James Version of Bible published
1614-1661 AD	James Guthrie, Covenanter minister
1625-1649 AD	Charles I, king of England, Scotland and Ireland
*1640 AD	**Kensie was born**
1649-1685 AD	Charles II, king of England, Scotland and Ireland
1654 AD	Castle Campbell burned
1701 AD	United Kingdom of Great Britain formed (England, Scotland and Wales)

*Print in colored pencil

"Make Your Own" Timeline Format

<u>MATERIALS</u>

Roll of white paper 8 to 12 inches wide or sheets of white paper

Tape or glue, pencil, colored pencils

<u>STEPS</u>

A time-line should be evenly spaced. An amount of space equals a certain period of time in history.

1. Using a ruler or yardstick, make a long horizontal line beginning near the open (left) end of the paper. (If you use sheets of paper, tape or glue several sheets together to make a roll.) The line should be in the center of the paper.

2. Make a mark on the line every <u>five</u> inches.

3. Make a vertical line about <u>two</u> inches long at each mark.

4. Beginning with the first line at the left end of the paper, label each with a date. <u>Pick the first date, such as 1600 B.C.</u> The time between each line is <u>fifty</u> years, so the next one would be <u>1550 B.C.</u> Remember, years labeled B.C. are counted **backward**!

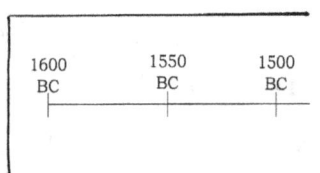

5. Label each mark until you write <u>0 B.C.</u>

6. The next line would be <u>50 A.D.</u> (Years labeled A.D. are counted **forward**.)   Label lines until you reach 2010 A.D.

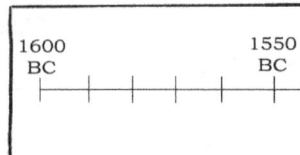

7. Return to the beginning of the time-line. Add smaller vertical lines at every inch along the line. Each space will be **ten** years.

8. Now you will add an event. Find the line for the date you want to document. Extend the line upward. At the bottom of the new line, write the specific date. At the top of the new line write the **text**.

Pictures to Color

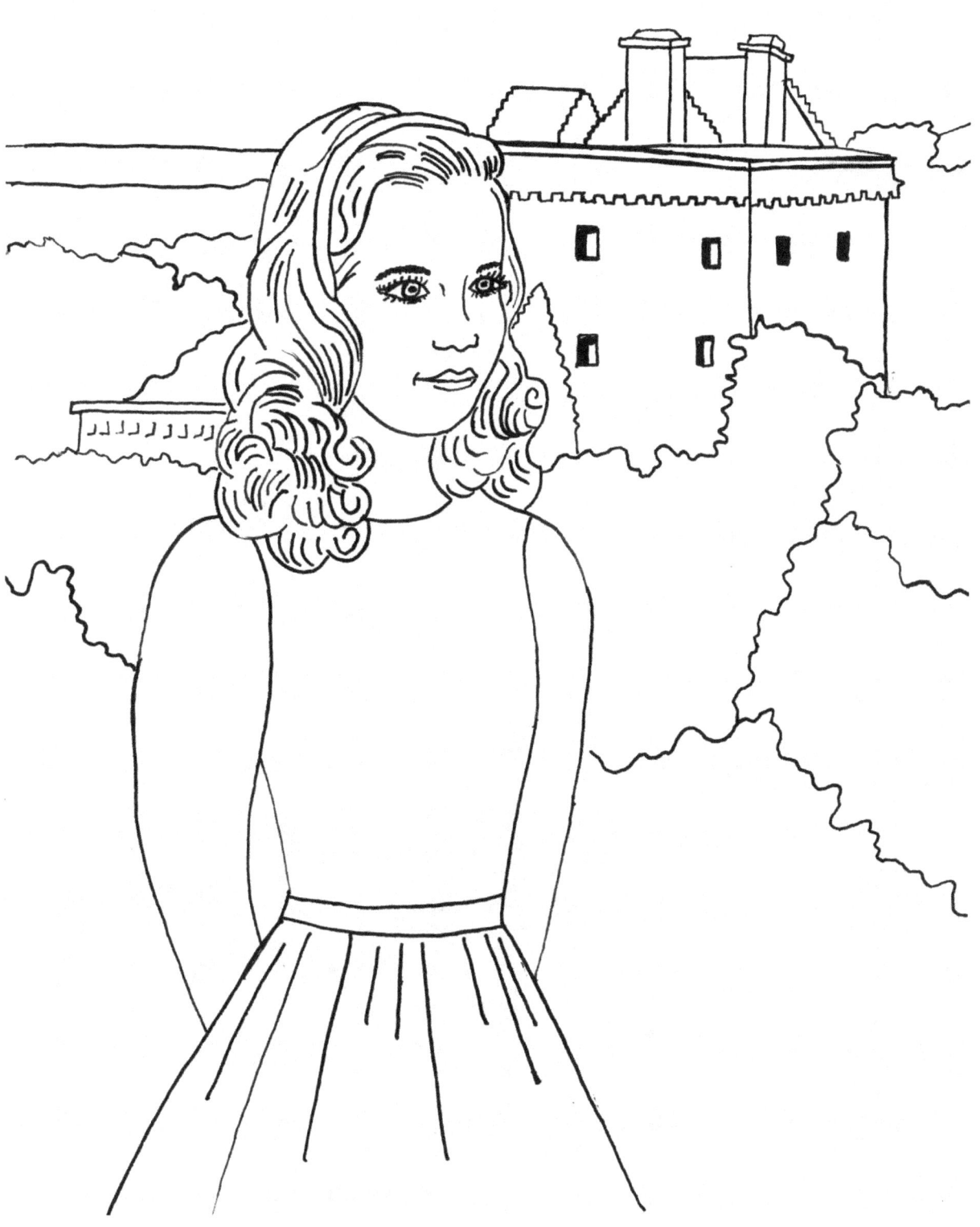

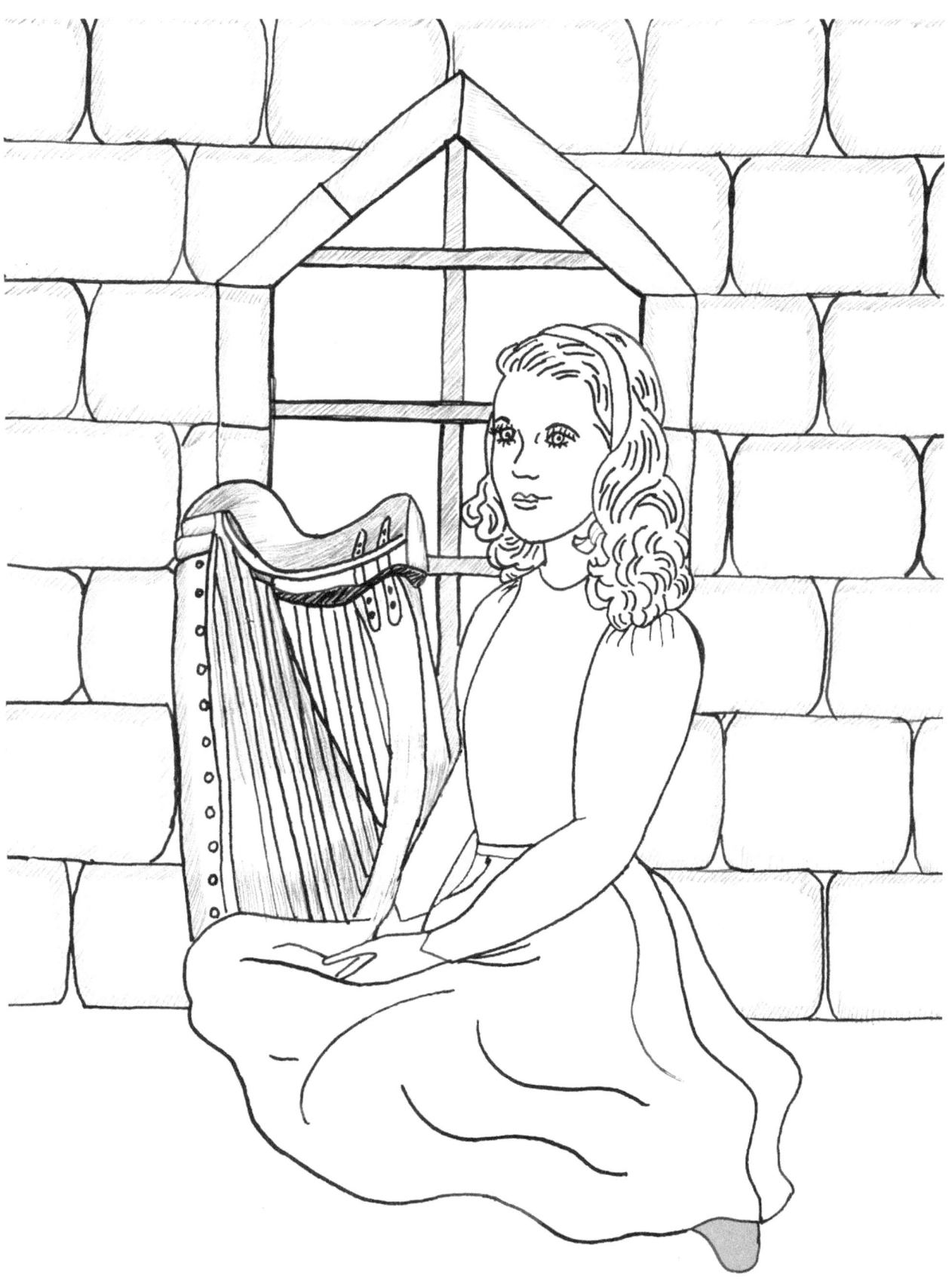

Keys and Answers

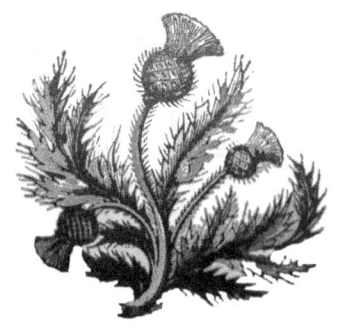

Crossword Solution

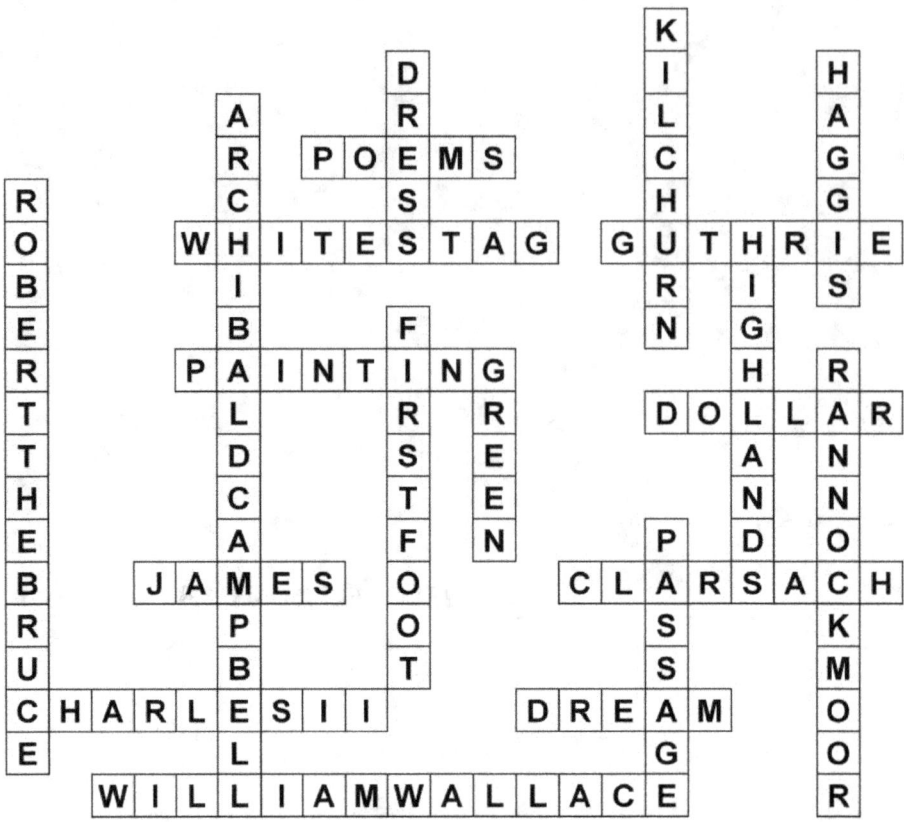

Review: Do You Know?

1. scarf
2. auburn
3. Gleume
4. haunted
5. great hall
6. Covenanters
7. MacGregor
8. Erica
9. Ceilidh
10. Hogmanay

11. bagpipe
12. bard
13. seaweed
14. tartan
15. haggis
16. coal
17. loch
18. fey
19. verses
20. locket

Talk About the Story

1. She found the scarf, she had seen her before

2. Brings good luck

5. A Gaelic harp. It was strung with brass and decorated with blue and green stones.

6. Guthrie castle was haunted and her family enjoyed stories about haunted castles

7. Write a special song and decide whether to wear the Campbell plaid

8. There were laws that allowed them to be killed because of their name

11. Archibald Campbell had attacked their castle so it was revenge. They were the future of the Campbells and would carry on the name.

13. He had blonde hair. The Vikings who attached Scotland long ago were blonde.

14. They are rare, few people see them. Legends say a sad one means sorrow in the future, seeing one means you are chosen.

15. Cold wind and snow. Kensie running and she heard angry voices. She smelled smoke and felt alone and afraid. Searched for something in the snow.

16. Celebration of New Years Eve. Clean everything. First Foot goes to other houses as blessing. Served haggis, dances, storyteller performed, sang, ate Black Bun.

Glossary

Bagpipe - A traditional Scottish instrument which is an airtight leather bag filled by a tube leading from the piper's mouth. Air escapes through a set of drones and a row of holes. It was used for dancing music and on the battlefield.

Bannockburn - A famous battle in which King Robert I (Bruce) and the Scots defeated the English leaving over thirty thousand killed.

Bard - professional poets who sang the praises of the chief and Scottish history. They inspired clansmen before battle, to celebrate victories, or at parties called ceilidhs.

Belted plaid - A combination of a kilt and plaid made of twelve ells of tartan cloth, pleated and fastened around the body with a belt.

Ceilidh - A traditional Scottish party of music, dancing and poetry by bards and storytellers.

Charles I - King of England, Scotland and Ireland (1625-1649) and son of King James. He was tried for treason and executed.

Charles II - King of England, Scotland, and Ireland (1649-1685) who was crowned at Scone in 1651.

Chief - The leader of a clan who commanded loyalty from clansmen. The father, law-giver, and judge of the clan.

Clan - An organization of people who share land, a name, and ancestral attachment.

Clarsach - A triangular Gaelic harp which stood upright and was played by striking strings made of brass or catgut with a quill or long fingernails.

Covenanter - A Scottish Presbyterian who supported the National Covenant or Solemn League and Covenant intended to defend and extend the Presbyterian church and religion.

Cromwell, Oliver - English soldier and statesman who supported demands for the execution of Charles I and ruthlessly suppressed rebellion of Scots.

Fiery Cross - Two pieces of wood burnt at upper end fastened to form a cross to which a rag dipped in sheep's blood was attached. Being burnt and bloody, the cross represented Fire and Sword.

Fire and Sword - An ordered and scheduled attack including destruction and killing.

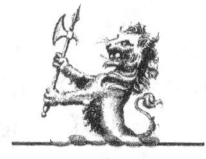

Haggis - A Scottish dish consisting of a mixture of minced sheep organs, oatmeal. fat, onions and seasonings and boiled in a sheep's stomach.

Highlands - A beautiful but inhospitable part of Scotland dominated by two mountain ranges.

Kilt - A knee-length skirt of woven wool with deep pleats and sewn to a strap. The ends of the fabric cross over each other in the front.

King James - James I of England and James VI of Scotland were the same person. He was the first to rule a "united" kingdom of England and Scotland.

Laird - Another name for the chief or leader of a clan.

Loch - An inland Scottish lake that lies quietly in a glen or winds between rocky hills. They are often arms of the open sea.

Loch Lomond - The largest fresh water lake which straddles the line between the Highlands and the Lowlands in Scotland. It was surrounded by native oak woods.

Plaid - A long rectangular piece of woolen cloth of a tartan pattern.

Robert the Bruce - Robert I of Scotland (1306-1329) who seized the crown and extended his control over Scotland. He won effective independence from England by his victory at Bannockburn.

Saffron - An orange-yellow dye made from dried crocus.

Scone - Village in central Scotland where Scottish kings were crowned. Early kings sat on the Stone of Scone also called the Stone of Destiny.

Tartan - A woven pattern of stripes of various widths and colors crossing at right angles against a solid background. Each forms a distinctive design worn by members of a particular Scottish clan.

Trews - Tartan cut crossways and worn tight to the skin in a form of pants or hose.

William Wallace - A Scottish noble, rebel leader and hero who led a rebellion against Edward I of England and captured Stirling Castle. He was proclaimed warden of Scotland but was eventually captured and executed.

Bibliography

Adam, Frank. *The Clans, Septs and Regiments of the Scottish Highlands.* Edinburgh: W and AK Johnson Limited, 1952

Astaire, Lesley and Martine, Roddy. *Living in the Highlands.* New York: Thames and Hudson Inc. 2000

Bingham, Caroline. *The Kings and Queens of Scotland.* New York: Taplinger Publishing Company, 1976

Douglas, Ronald MacDonald. *Scottish Lore and Folklore.* New York: Beekman House, 1982

Fisher, Andrew. *A Traveler's History of Scotland.* New York: Interlink Publishing Group, 2000

Fry, Plantagent and Somerset, Fiona. *The History of Scotland.* London: Routledge and Kegan Paul, 1982

Grant, Neil. *Scottish Clans and Tartans.* New York: The Lyons Press, 2000

Grimble, Ian. *Clans and Chiefs.* Edinburgh: Blond and Briggs, 2000

Herman, Arthur. *How the Scots Invented the Modern World.* New York: Crown Publishers, 2001

Linklater, Eric. *The Survival of Scotland.* Garden City, NY: Doubleday and Company, 1968

MacKinnon, Charles. *Scottish Highlanders.* New York: Barnes and Noble, 1984

Macleod, John. *Dynasty: The Stuarts 1560-1807.* New York: St. Martin's Press, 1999

Magnusson, Magnus. *Scotland: The Story of a Nation.* New York: Atlantic Monthly Press, 2000

McKerral, Andrew. *The Clan Campbell.* Edenburg: W and AK Johnson and GW Bacon Ltd., 1962

Menzies, Gordon. *In Search of Scotland.* Lanham, MD: Roberts Rinehart Publishers, 2001

Bibliography Continued.

Moncreiffe, Sir Iain. *The Highland Clans.* New York: Clarkson N. Potter, Inc., 1967

Montgomery-Massingbird, Hugh and Sykes, Christopher Simon. *Great Houses of Scotland.* New York: Rizzoli International Publications Inc. 1997

Ramsay, Paul. *Lochs and Glens of Scotland.* New York: Cross River Press, 1994

Wood, John Philip. *The Peerage of Scotland. Volume 1.* Edinburgh: George Ramsay and Company, 1993

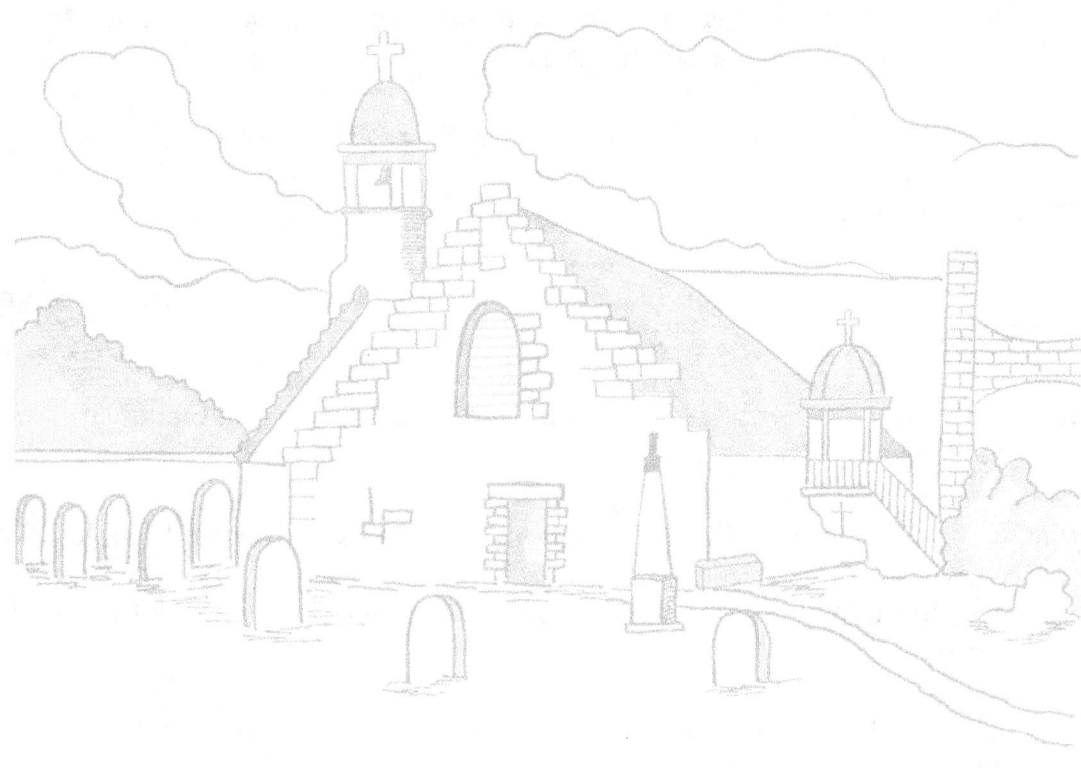

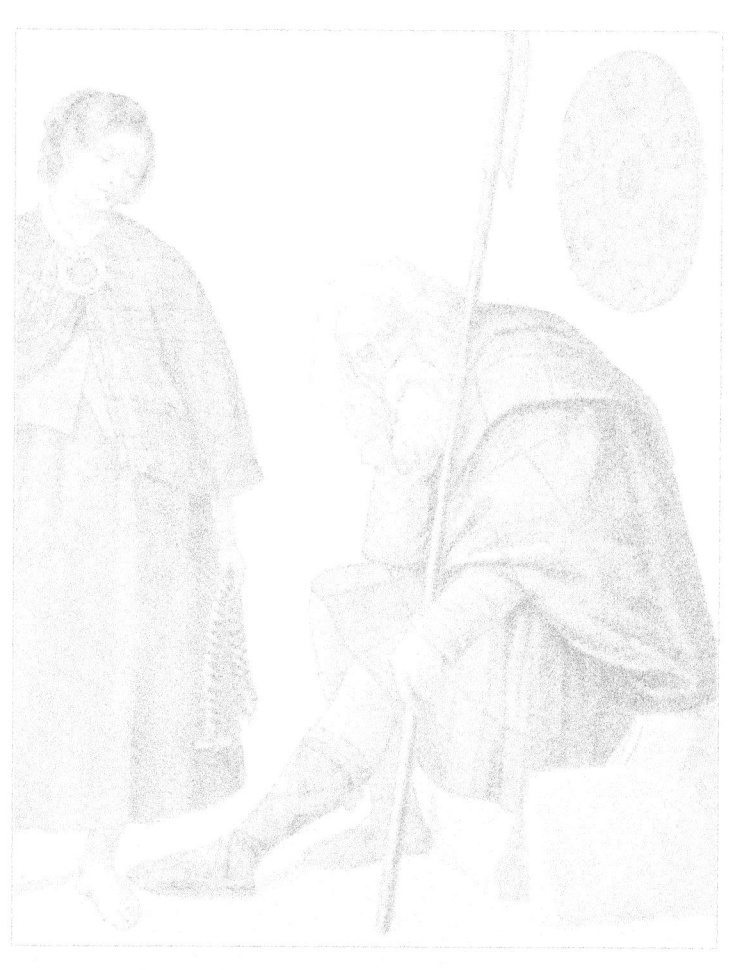